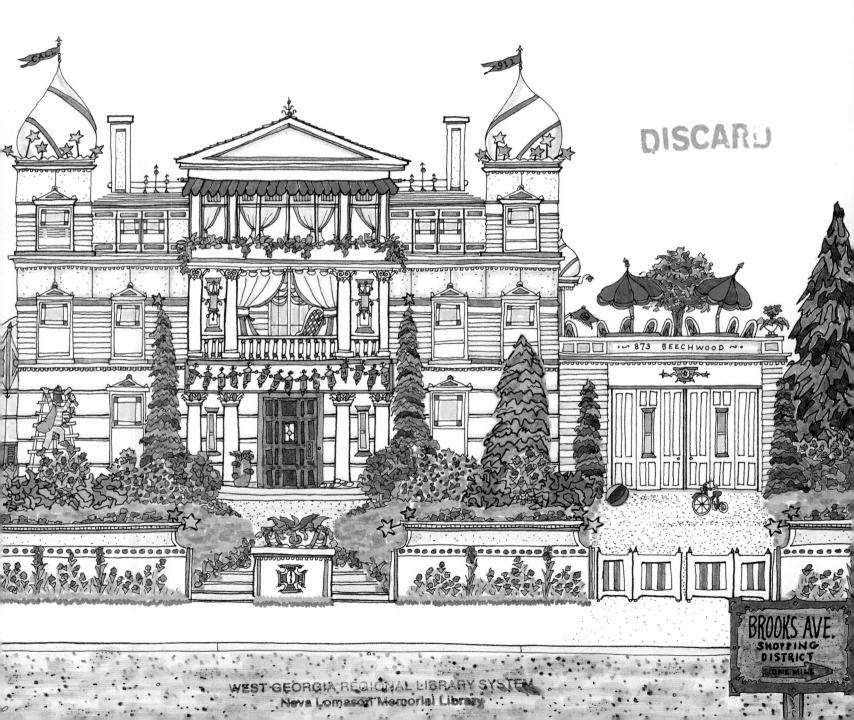

POLICE PATROL

Katherine K. Winkleman
Illustrations by John S. Winkleman

Walker and Company
New York

For our son, Pendray, who reminds us that apples can grow on orange trees, mice like to wear top hats, and dragons do sing.

Special thanks to Officer Adam D'Amico, Officer James Docherty, Corrections Officer Sally Graham, Officer Erica Brown, Captain Mike Whalen, Denise Villand, and the New York City Police Museum; their vital guidance and knowledge helped shape *Police Patrol*. And, our deep gratitude to our editor, Emily Easton, and our family, our friends, and our clients for their support and patience.

Thank you, Pennsylvania Police Commissioner Richard Neal, Sergeant Archer, P.O. Borbidge, Captain Burton, P.O. John Cannon, Sergeant Gerry Grdinich, William Huber, Joseph McBride, and Sergeant Mike Vitale.

Thank you, New York City P.O. Bill Church, Sergeant Jim Cowan, P.O. Peter Curtin, P.O. Ed D'Alessandro, P.O. Joe Danaher, Captain John Dowie, Detective Peter Dziuk, Bill Edgehill, Captain George F. Farrell, P.O. Brendon Galligan, Sergeant John Geist, P.O. John Harkins, Lieutenant Helfand, P.O. Jim Hennessy, P.O. Daniel Ingoldsby, P.O. Raymond Mancini and his police dog Jake, P.O. Vincent Martinez, Detective McCabe, P.O. Brian McGowan, Lieutenant Richard Messemer, Detective Sergeant Joseph Noschese, P.O. Mike O'Brien, P.O. Dominick Palermo, Lieutenant Roger Parrino, P.O. Joseph Perno and his horse Kevin Levin, P.O. Stephen Petrillo, John Podracky, P.O. Terry Riordan, P.O. Sacco, Sergeant William Toohey, Sergeant Nick Villand, Captain William Wilkens, and P.O. David Yat.

First published in the United States of America in 1996 by Walker Publishing Company, Inc.
Published simultaneously in Canada by Thomas Allen & Son Canada, Limited, Markham, Ontario
Library of Congress Cataloging-in-Publication Data
Winkleman, Katherine K.
Police Patrol/Katherine K. Winkleman; illustrations by John S. Winkleman
p. cm.
Includes index.
Summary: Describes the activities that take place at a police station and the duties of different types of officers.
ISBN 0-8027-8453-4 (hardcover). —ISBN 0-8027-8454-2 (reinforced binding)
1. Police—Juvenile literature. [1. Police.] I. Winkleman, HV7922.W53 1996
363.2'32—dc20
96-10761
CIP
AC

Book design by Diane Stevenson of Snap-Haus Graphics
Printed in Hong Kong
2 4 6 8 10 9 7 5 3 1

POLICE

"5-Adam-Boy, 5-Adam-Boy. We have a police officer who needs backup — Priority 1, on 873 Beechwood, suspected burglar," says the police dispatcher over the patrol car radio. 5-Adam and 5-Boy cars immediately respond to the call.

IN MANY SQUAD CARS THERE'S AN ELECTRONIC MAP THAT SHOWS POLICE EXACTLY WHERE TO GO TO RESPOND TO A 911 CALL.

POLICE STATION

The police officers bring in the burglar and book him. After they fingerprint and photograph him, the officers give all the information to the desk sergeant. The burglar will stay in the holding cell until a police van brings him to jail to wait for his bail hearing in court.

Desk Sergeant

PROPERTY ☆ ROOM

EVIDENCE ☆ ROOM

Fingerprinting area

FINGER PRINTING

Holding cell

Mug shot

The criminal's gun is unloaded by holding it inside the gunport and opening it. In case the gun fires, the bullet will harmlessly drop to the bottom.

Gunport

The detectives' office is located away from the public area so that they can concentrate on investigations and meet with witnesses and victims in private.

When officers are not eating in the multipurpose room, it can be used for other things, such as showing witnesses mug shots of local criminals, or meeting with community leaders to discuss problems.

Detectives' office

Multipurpose room

Mug shot book

Muster room

Before each shift or tour begins, officers gather in the muster room. The lieutenant informs them of any police news and assigns them to a patrol area for the day.

PATROL OFFICERS

Both men and women can be police officers. Their job is "to protect and to serve" the public. In most police departments, over half of the staff are patrol officers. Each officer works with a partner to safeguard the community. Police officers patrol on foot and in squad cars, on motorized scooters, and in other vehicles — even on bicycles.

Police hats have a special plastic holder. In it, many officers place a photo of their family, or of an officer who died in the line of duty.

Patrol officers wear uniforms so they can be easily seen by the public. Uniforms also help in crime prevention. If criminals see police, they usually won't commit a crime.

Two-way radio/shoulder mike

Memo book
(in back pocket)

Pens

Shield

Extra bullets

Flashlight
(not shown)

Mace
(not
shown)

Bulletproof
vest
(under shirt)

Whistle

9mm gun

Handcuffs

Baton
or
night-
stick

Sam Browne gun belt

Because each officer carries only one pair of metal handcuffs,

plastic throwaway handcuffs are often used when many people are arrested at once.

ARRESTING THE SUSPECT

Arresting a suspect can often be difficult and dangerous, yet officers use their guns only when there is no other choice. Officers always try to make sure that no one is hurt during an arrest.

A police officer's best weapon is his voice. In many situations, the perpetrator, or "perp," can be talked into giving himself up.

MIRANDA WARNING

When a suspect is being arrested, the police officer reads the Miranda warning, which tells the prisoner what rights he or she has. If the Miranda warning is not read to the prisoner, the court will let him or her go free.

Miranda Warning

- You have the right to remain silent and refuse to answer questions.
- Anything you do say may be used against you in a court of law.
- You have the right to consult an attorney before speaking to the police and to have an attorney present during any questioning now or in the future.
- If you cannot afford an attorney, one will be provided for you without cost.
- If you do not have an attorney available, you have the right to remain silent until you have had an opportunity to consult with one.
- Now that I have advised you of your rights, are you willing to answer questions?

CORRECTIONAL INSTITUTIONS

The proper word for *prison* is *correctional institution*. These institutions keep dangerous criminals away from the public. Corrections officers guard the high concrete walls to prevent inmates from escaping. Guards do not carry guns unless there is an emergency.

EASTON CORRECTIONAL INSTITUTION

After a car drives into the sally port, the doors automatically shut in front of the car and behind it to prevent escape.

BEWARE

POLICE
DIAL 911

CAUTION

Inmates are taught job skills and receive special counseling to help them learn to live in society and obey its laws. Some prisoners study hard and receive high school and college diplomas.

Instead of going to jail, some criminals are placed under house arrest, which means they cannot leave their homes. If they try to escape, the electronic bracelet they wear gives off a signal to warn the police.

DETECTIVES

Detectives investigate crimes. Whether it is a bank robbery, a house break-in, or a murder, the detectives look for clues to answer the questions who, what, when, where, why, and how.

Detectives use everyday items like tweezers, pens, plastic bags, and even magnifying glasses to help with an investigation.

To solve the crime, detectives search the scene, look at physical evidence, interview witnesses, and review the criminal's methods (called modus operandi, or MO for short).

The crime scene is taped off and guarded because anyone walking through it might leave trace evidence behind (like a hair or a footprint) which might be mistaken for the criminal's. A crime photographer takes pictures to record the scene.

CRIME LAB

As the crime scene unit gathers evidence (such as hair, blood, jewelry, or broken glass), each clue is packaged separately in a plastic bag and labeled. Detectives bring the samples to the police crime lab, where scientists analyze them. This analysis is often more important evidence than a suspect's confession.

Along with fingerprints and photographs, genetic fingerprinting is considered to provide vital evidence. Using special machinery and chemicals, a "DNA print" is created from blood, hair roots, or skin samples.

FINGERPRINTS

Since no two people have exactly the same fingerprints, they are important clues. In the past, a suspect would be fingerprinted using ink. Now many stations use finger imaging, a method of scanning fingers electronically to create fingerprint cards.

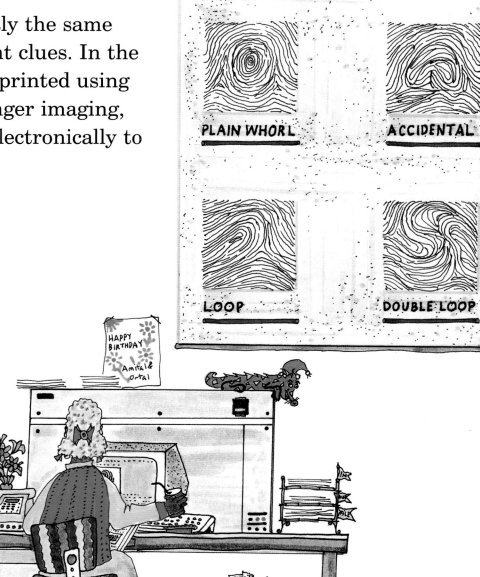

PLAIN WHORL

ACCIDENTAL

LOOP

DOUBLE LOOP

Technicians use computers to compare the thousands of fingerprints on file to the sample prints. Once the machines have found potential matches, the technician looks at each print for similar patterns of arches, loops, and whorls.

HIGHWAY PATROL

The highway patrol uses police cars, motorcycles, and even snowmobiles to enforce traffic laws, assist drivers who need help, and catch suspects. Patrol cars have powerful motors and special reinforced tires that prevent skidding during high-speed chases.

Sometimes an aviation unit is called to help the highway patrol catch a suspect.

AVIATION

One of the best ways to search is by air. Helicopters are able to hover in one place and fly low to the ground.

They are equipped with special infrared cameras that can find hidden suspects. These cameras detect body heat, which shows up as red against the green background on the monitor.

Infrared video camera

Spotlight

TIMBER LODGE
HOME OF THE FRESHEST SALMON

closed

~⊙~
WATCH THIS SITE
ON THIS SITE A MODERN AND
EFFICIENT FAST FOOD/GASOLINE
STATION WILL BE BUILT TO EASE
~ YOUR TRAVELS ~

YOUR HIGHWAY DOLLARS AT WORK

HARBOR AND SCUBA UNITS

In areas that have oceans, rivers, or large lakes, the police force includes harbor units and scuba units. Harbor police patrol the waters to make sure that people are boating safely. They also rescue drowning people.

The scuba unit combs the bottom of the water for guns and other evidence that criminals toss away. It also works with the harbor unit to inspect boats suspected of smuggling drugs or other illegal goods.

A longer version of the same "fish" was used to locate a sunken luxury ocean liner, the *Titanic*.

Drug smugglers often hide drugs by attaching them to the bottom of a ship. The scuba unit will guide a robot "fish" under the ship to record and send sonar images of the hull through its video camera to the police boat. Then a police scuba diver will swim below the hull to check any suspicious objects.

Suspicious object

MOUNTED POLICE

Seated upon tall horses are the mounted police. They can be found in the country, in towns, and even in cities. Sitting so high allows the mounted patrol officer to see above the heads of a crowd to spot any trouble.

When an officer and horse are on crowd control duty, a flick of the officer's reins tells the horse whether to back up, swing its hindquarters around, or move sideways, pushing a crowd of people out of the way.

A lanyard connects the officer's gun to his uniform to keep the gun from falling out.

Lanyard

O'REILLY

THE ALLEN-STEVENSON School

P.S. 158

SUMMIT LANE School

POLICE DO NOT CROSS

Mounted police are sometimes called "9-foot cops" because if they were measured while riding on a horse, they would be nine feet tall!

CANINE PARTNERS

The saying that a dog is a man's best friend applies 100 percent in the canine division, where an officer's partner is a police dog.

Police dogs obey their human partners without question. They are trained to follow the scent trail of suspects, sniff out hidden drugs, detect illegal food in airports, attack and disarm dangerous criminals, and perform many other police duties that may be too risky for their human partners.

When police dogs retire, their human partners often adopt them as family pets.

BOMB SQUAD

Wearing 75 to 100 pounds of protective gear, each bomb squad member searches the building for the suspected bomb, or "device," which could be hidden anywhere. Highly trained bomb squad dogs are used to sniff out explosives.

A worker helps the squad by pointing out any object that does not belong—for instance, a wastepaper basket that was never there before.

First the entire building is emptied of people, except for the squad members. Then a remote-controlled robot can be used to inspect, disarm, or detonate the bomb.

Bomb squad members wear only cotton, leather, or rubber clothing. Other materials, such as polyester, generate static electricity, which may set off the device.

POLICE

If the bomb can be removed, it is often carefully placed in a specially woven wicker container and moved a safe distance away. When the bomb explodes, the gases and pressure are released, but the wicker keeps the shrapnel from escaping.

UNDERCOVER POLICE

Not all police officers wear uniforms. Some are undercover—that is, they're in disguise, so they blend in with the other people around them. Sometimes they look like a friendly neighbor, grandmother, or florist. Sometimes they look like criminals.

Undercover police offi[cer]

Undercover police officer

Undercover officers often solve cases just by watching, listening, and waiting. They might be undercover for only a day or may be on the same stakeout for months, depending on how important and complicated the investigation is.

Undercover police officer

SPECIAL FORCES AND SWAT TEAMS

When people need help, they call the police. When the police need help, they call "special forces." These officers are trained in complicated rescues, hostage negotiations, and dangerous raids, and they help in major disasters such as earthquakes and floods. Special forces responsibilities are divided between Special Weapons and Tactics ("SWAT") teams and other highly trained units.

FBI AND STATE POLICE

In large disasters or serious criminal situations, the local police are often joined by state police and federal law enforcement agencies, which may include the Federal Bureau of Investigation (FBI), the Bureau of Alcohol, Tobacco and Firearms (ATF), and the Secret Service.

SMALL TOWNS

In a small town, there might be one police chief or sheriff and a couple of deputies. Each officer is responsible for patrols, traffic enforcement, investigation, and catching criminals. Everyone in the community knows the officers well and no one hesitates to ask for their help, even if it is simply to rescue a cat.

Many communities hire "public safety directors" to be in charge of the police, the fire department, and rescue services.

NICHOLAS

KIDS PLAY SPACE

WELCOME OUR Public Safety Director

TOWN H

CHARLES Drug Store est. 1927

Lil's LUNCH DESSERTS

Barber

KIDS

BOOKS

Rx

WELCOME

POLICE DEPARTMENT

Escaped HERMIT CRAB Call PHILLIP

OPEN

COUNTY SHERIFF

BEHIND THE SCENES

Police work depends on cooperation between officers on the front line and the many officers and civilians behind the scenes. Computer technicians, police academy instructors, police dispatchers, telephone operators, secretaries, and many others are essential for catching criminals.

Police dispatchers in big cities might have ten or fifteen emergency calls coming in at once. They need to determine how serious each emergency is, assign police (and send ambulances when needed), and keep speaking with all the different callers.

REMEMBER ★ YOUR ★ CODES

10-4 Acknowledgement

10-5 Repeat Message

10-10 Possible crime
(prowler, suspicious person / vehicle, shots fired, etc...)

10-12 P.O. HOLDING SUSPECT

10-13 ASSIST POLICE OFFICER

10-16 Vehicle reporte stolen

10-50 Disorderly pers

BE SAFE—BE ALERT

1. Never pick up a gun, even if it looks like a toy. Go tell your parents, a police officer, or another grown-up, or dial 911.
2. If a stranger tries to talk to you, get away and tell a grown-up immediately.
3. When playing outside, team up with a buddy so if there's trouble, you're not alone.
4. When you're in a car, make sure *everyone's* seat belt is fastened. Even if the kids have fastened theirs, many grown-ups forget their own.
5. Always ask a grown-up first before you touch any animal, including a dog or cat.
6. Kids *and* grown-ups should cross the street only at the intersection and if the sign says "walk." No matter what, always look both ways before crossing.
7. Don't open the door to strangers.
8. Always tell your parents or your teacher where you are going or playing.
9. Never touch firecrackers.
10. Never try illegal drugs or use another person's prescription drugs.

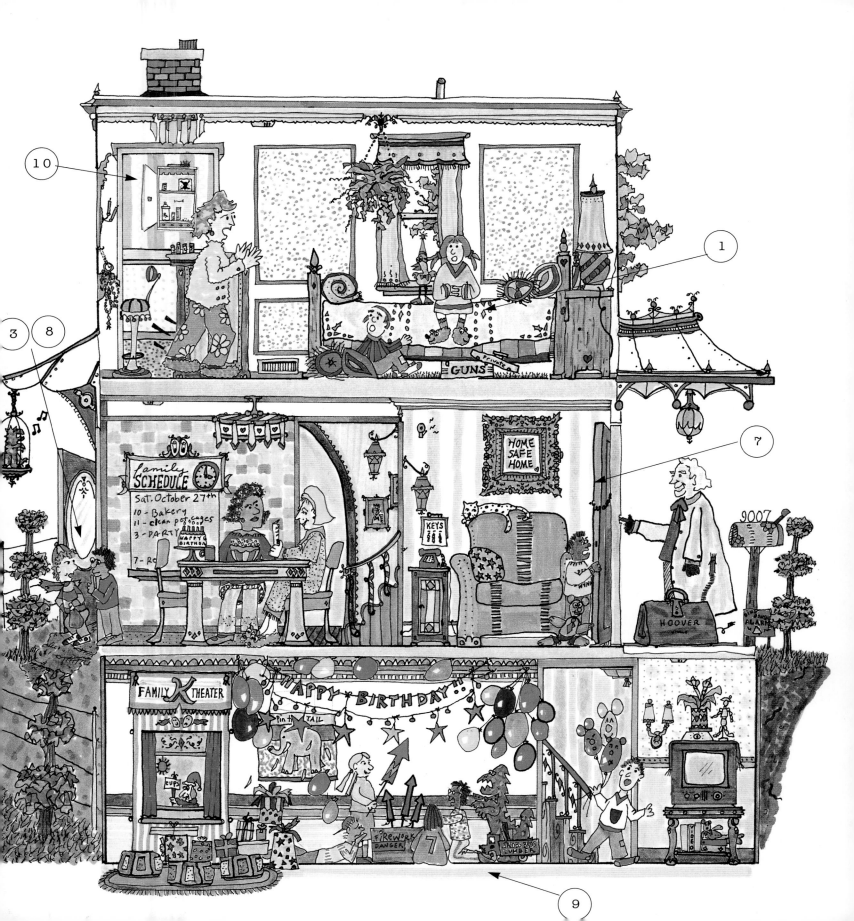

DIAL
911   POLICE